ISBN 1 85103 074 3

First published 1988 by Editions Gallimard
First published 1989 in Great Britain by Moonlight Publishing Ltd,
36 Stratford Road, London W8
© 1988 Editions Gallimard
English text © 1989 Moonlight Publishing Ltd

Printed in Italy by La Editoriale Libraria

THE DISCOVERY
OF THE WORLD
VOL 2: NAVIGATORS AND EXPLORERS

DISCOVERERS

Written and illustrated by
François Place

Translated by Margaret Malpas

MOONLIGHT PUBLISHING

Contents

A Chronology of Exploration

3500 B.C.
Egyptian boats.
2000-1500 B.C.
Sailors from Crete
and Phoenicia.
800 B.C.
Homer's *Odyssey*.
350-330 B.C.
Voyages of Pytheas.
2nd century A.D.
Ptolemy drew his
maps.
610 Beginning of
Islam.
800 Viking raids into
Europe.
982 Erik the Red
reached Greenland.
12th century Most
boats steered by a
rudder at the stern.
1336-1341 First
voyages to the
Canaries.
1405-1433 The
Chinese admiral
Cheng Ho went to
Indonesia, India,
Arabia and the east
coast of Africa.
1432 Gil Eannes
rounded Cape
Bojador.

1454 Gutenberg's
Bible, the first book
printed with movable
lead type.
1488 Bartholomew
Dias rounded the
Cape of Storms
(Cape of Good
Hope).

1492 Columbus
reached the
Caribbean (Cuba
and Hispaniola).
1494 Treaty of
Tordesillas.
1497 John Cabot
sailed past Labrador.

1497-1499 Vasco da
Gama went round the
southern tip of Africa
to India.
1500 Pedro Cabral
landed in Brazil.
1511 The Portuguese
conquered Malacca.
1519 Cortez set sail
for Mexico.
1519 First voyage
round the world, by
Magellan and
de Elcano.
1524 Verrazano
explored the north-
east coast of America.
1534 Jacques Cartier
explored the
St Lawrence.
1543 The Portuguese
arrived in Japan.

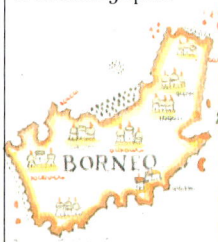

BORNEO

1552 Las Casas wrote of the 'destruction of the Indies'.

1578 Sir Francis Drake in the Pacific on the second voyage round the world.

1594-1597 Barents discovered Spitzbergen and Novaya Zemlya while trying to find the North-east Passage.

1615 Baffin sailed to the west of Greenland.

1616 Le Maire and Schouten sailed round Cape Horn.

1642-1644 Tasman's voyage in search of the southern continent. He found Van Diemen's Land (Tasmania).

1650-1697 The golden age of piracy in the West Indies.

1725-1728 Bering was sent by the Tsar to find the North-east Passage. He discovered the Bering Strait between Asia and America.

1731 The sextant was invented.

1766-1768 Wallis sailed to Oceania.

1768-1769 Bougainville sailed the Pacific and found Tahiti.

1768-1771 Cook's first voyage. He found New Zealand and explored the east coast of Australia.

1772-1775 Cook's second voyage in search of the southern continent. He sailed round the Antarctic.

1776-1779 Cook's third voyage. He explored the islands of the Pacific and found Hawaii; he then went north, and tried to reach the North-west Passage through the Bering Strait.

1785-1788 La Pérouse went to Asia, North America and the western Pacific.

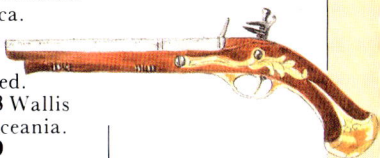

1839-1841 Ross tried to reach Antarctica.

1839-1840 Dumont d'Urville went to Antarctica and found Adélie Land.

1878 Nordenskjöld sailed through the North-east Passage.

1903-1906 Amundsen sailed through the North-west Passage.

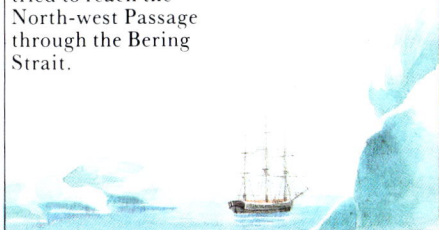

Odysseus

Greek ships of the 6th century B.C.

To escape from the Cyclops Polyphemus, Odysseus and his companions put out his single eye. Mad with pain and rage, Polyphemus hurled rocks after them as they fled.

After fighting in the Greek army which conquered Troy, Odysseus made a bad mistake: he annoyed Poseidon, the god of the sea, who decided to punish him by preventing him from reaching his homeland.

So for ten long years Odysseus wandered, sometimes helped and sometimes hindered by the gods. On his way he had many adventures. He encountered the Sirens, who tried to lure his ship on to the rocks; the Cyclops; the man-eating Laestrygonians; the Lotus-eaters; the monster Scylla and the whirlpool Charybdis; Circe the enchantress, who turned his sailors into pigs; the nymph Calypso; the princess Nausicaa – a whole cavalcade of imaginary characters.

The *Odyssey*, written in Greece about 3,000 years ago by the blind poet Homer, is the first great 'traveller's tale'.

To escape the tempting song of the Sirens, Odysseus ordered his men to tie him to the ship's mast.

Seafarers of the Ancient World

Long before the time of Homer, various civilisations grew up around the Mediterranean. Cretans, Egyptians and Phoenicians built ships for many purposes: fishing, trade, war, even piracy. Travel by sea was an important part of life, but sailors were very cautious; they tried to avoid going out of sight of land, and at night they furled their sails and anchored their ships close to the shore.

Greek sailors hauling on the rigging

Egyptian ship

Sailors and fishermen of these times did not think of dolphins as fish; they were friends. The Greeks believed that the sea-gods rode on dolphins, and used them as messengers.

By the 5th century B.C., Greek scholars were convinced that the earth was a sphere, though for centuries no one believed them. Most people thought that the earth was a flat plate, and that anyone who went too far might fall off the edge.

Erastothenes (3rd century B.C.) was the first scientific geographer. Ptolemy was the first great map-maker; he drew this map in the 2nd century A.D.

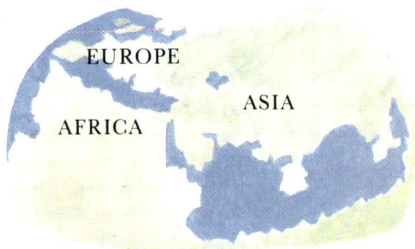

Beyond the Pillars of Hercules (which we now call the Strait of Gibraltar) stretched the vast ocean. Sailors used to the sheltered Mediterranean found the open seas very alarming. But the Phoenicians very early learned how to reach the islands of the Celts, in the North Atlantic, to obtain the tin they needed to make bronze.

There are many tales of attempts to discover 'the world' – some no doubt

as much fantasy as fact. For instance, some Phoenicians sent by the Pharaoh Nechao claimed to have sailed right round Africa. But in about 330 B.C. Pytheas, a Greek sailor from Marseilles, actually did sail right up the coast of England and Scotland, and reached the mysterious kingdom of Thule – possibly the Shetlands, or even Iceland.

The most important contribution which these sailors made to our history was not so much their voyages as the development of their great maritime cities: Knossos, Tyre, Athens, Carthage, Alexandria, Ostia. These cities grew up around harbours, and became rich through trading in goods carried across the seas.

The lighthouse at Alexandria was one of the seven wonders of the world.

Phoenician trading-ship

A Greek galley could travel extremely fast. It had a long narrow hull, a square sail, and several banks of oars.

The Vikings

At the end of the 8th century, men from the north landed on the British coast and began a campaign which carried them over much of Europe. As they advanced, they sailed up the big rivers and pillaged any settlement they found: They were the Vikings.

They were superb ship-builders. Their fighting ship, the drakkar, was long and light, riding high on the water and skimming over the waves, rowed by between 30 and 50 warriors. It had a removable mast and a square sail, to be used when the wind was favourable.

The Vikings also built knarrs, heavier ships strong enough to carry large loads for long distances. These were used to transport whole families and their belongings and cattle to a new life in the Viking colonies.

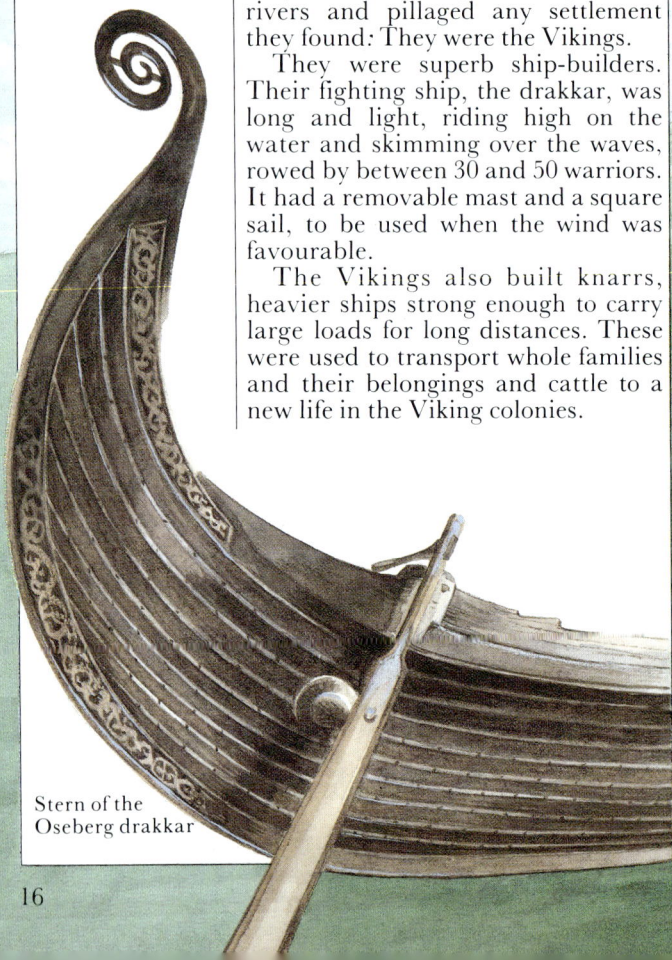

Stern of the Oseberg drakkar

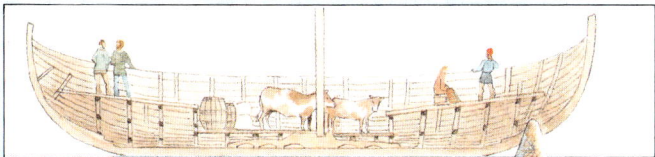

Section of a knarr

*'From the fury of the Norsemen,
good Lord deliver us,'*
ran a prayer of the time.

Viking warrior

The Vikings decorated many of their possessions with twining patterns and imaginary animals. On the prow of the drakkar they carried a fearsome dragon's head, to terrorise their enemies.

After little more than two centuries, the Vikings were established from England to Sicily. They competed with the Arabs for trade in the Mediterranean; they ruled Kiev and Novgorod in Russia; and they traded over the whole area between the Baltic and Constantinople. They set up colonies in the Atlantic, and explored the Faeroes, Shetland and Iceland. In 982, Erik the Red left Iceland and set sail for Greenland.

All these sea-voyages needed much experience of the oceans: knowledge of winds and currents, and an ability to predict changes in the weather. The Vikings steered at night by using the Pole Star to find the north. In their sagas, the long poems about their adventures, they describe how they even navigated in fog, using the 'sun-stone', possibly a mineral called cordierite. All in all, their navigational techniques were immensely sophisticated.

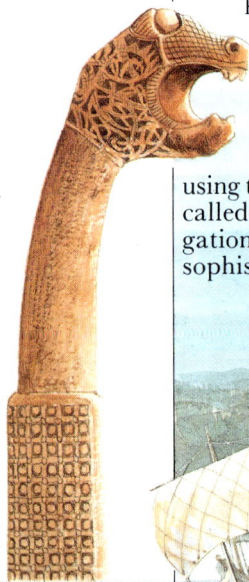

In 1001 Leif Eriksson, son of Erik the Red, left Greenland and sailed to Newfoundland, or Vinland, as the Vikings called it. He landed at a place now called L'Anse aux Meadows. The Vikings stayed in America for only twenty years; but they were the first Europeans to reach the New World, five centuries before Columbus.

Once the warriors had taken control of an area, the settlers followed, to establish a new Viking colony there.

This picture from the Bayeux Tapestry shows William the Conqueror and his men landing in England aboard their Viking ships.

Early ships and sails

Carvel-built boat
(Mediterranean)

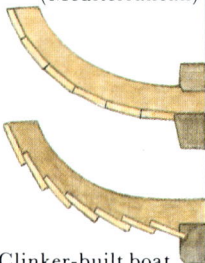

Clinker-built boat
(northern Europe)

By the 12th century, ships from northern Europe were quite different from those in the south. The main type of ship in the Mediterranean, for both war and trade, was still the galley, just as it had been for hundreds of years. Galleys could move very fast, and as they had oars as well as sails, they were not much delayed by lack of wind. Most of them had lateen (triangular) sails, so that they could be sailed very close to the wind, though they were tricky to manoeuvre. Galleys continued to follow their long-established trade routes across the seas, right up to the 17th century.

Traders in the north, however, sailed sturdy cargo boats called cogs. The cities on the Baltic and North Sea coasts were grouped together to form a trading community, the Hanse. Navigation was more difficult here than in the Mediterranean; sandbanks, currents, and shallow channels navigable only at high tide made the work of the official pilots absolutely vital. They used a lead to check the depth of the water as they guided the cogs through the dangerous waters.

The Basques introduced the cog into the Mediterranean, where it revolutionised ship design.

The cog's rudder was at the stern, instead of on the starboard side. Its sail was square, and could be reefed in to make it smaller.

Carracks, big cargo-ships with three or four masts, brought trade and wealth to the large medieval ports, which were now fortified for protection.

The Arabs
and the monsoon

Arab
astrolabe

The Arabs were
skilled astronomers.
Their astrolabe,
a remarkable
instrument used to
make astronomical
observations, was the
basis of many
instruments used in
navigation.

From Madagascar to the Coromandel
Coast, Arab dhows from the Red Sea
and the Persian Gulf dominated the
Indian Ocean.

After the Turks closed the land-
routes from Asia to Europe, the spice
trade passed through Egypt, making
the fortunes of merchants in Cairo and
Alexandria.

The key to navigation in the Indian
Ocean is the monsoon, a strong wind
which blows towards the land in
summer and away from it in winter.
Long before the Portuguese arrived
there, Persian and Arab sailors who
understood the monsoons had set up
trading-posts in India; their most
skilled navigators, the Mull Alim,
were universally respected for their
knowledge of the sea. In 1450 the most
famous of them, Ibn Majid, wrote a
guide to the Red Sea and the Indian

Ocean; it is so accurate that it can still be used today. Ibn Majid may well have been the pilot who guided Vasco da Gama's ships on his first voyage to India.

The story of Sinbad the Sailor was a warning to anyone who thought of sailing these waters without an experienced pilot. Sinbad was a merchant from Baghdad who sailed east many times to bring back spices. He became rich, but had many hair-raising adventures during his voyages.

On one of his voyages, Sinbad's ship moored beside an island, and all the sailors went ashore. Suddenly the 'island' started to move! The terrified sailors had to rush back on board; it was not an island at all, but a huge whale.

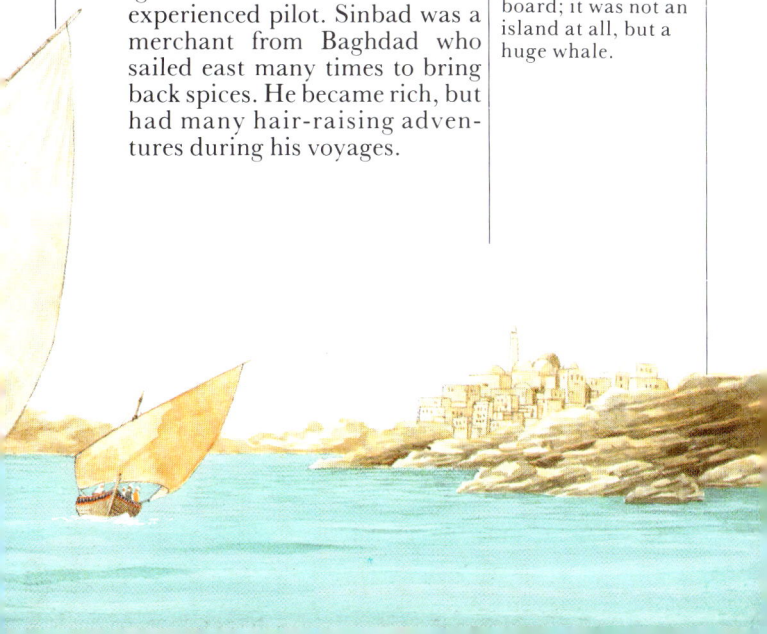

Sea-legends of the Middle Ages

The Sirens of Greek mythology, half-woman, half-bird, were the origin of the mermaids of legend and folklore. Travellers were sometimes attracted to, sometimes repulsed by mermaids with fish tails. They often prophesied storms or disasters. Many sailors, including Christopher Columbus, claimed to have seen them.

At the beginning of the 15th century, few sailors were brave enough to venture out into the open ocean, an alarming expanse which the early map-makers had filled with the imaginary places and strange creatures described in folk-tales and legends.

One of the earliest stories describes the voyage made by a 5th-century Irish monk, St Brendan. On his way he visited the Paradise of the Birds, the Island of Fruit, and the Island of Eternal Life – all in the North Atlantic. The tale fitted in with the medieval idea of Paradise: an inaccessible island somewhere at the far side of the ocean. It was often marked on medieval maps.

An ancient print showing St Brendan and his companions meeting a mermaid.

A medieval view of the whale

During the Middle Ages, a few scholars were convinced that the Earth was round, but no one could be persuaded to prove it; sailors lacked the ships and the navigation skills to undertake such a long voyage. Ordinary sailors were quite certain that the sea boiled at the Equator, and that they were much more likely to find the Great Sea Serpent, Leviathan, than the Fortunate Isles.

Terrified by these legendary perils, no one was prepared to travel beyond the 'known' world; true exploration could not begin until courageous sailors overcame their fear and set sail for the unknown.

The Fortunate Isles.

The dreadful sea-monster Leviathan

The beginning of map-making

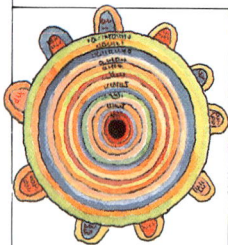

Ptolemy's universe, with the earth at the centre. When he drew maps he used a network of lines, rather like our lines of latitude and longitude, to help him to put things in the right places.

Medieval *mappa mundi* (map of the world)

Map-makers in the Middle Ages were more interested in producing a picture of the world which corresponded with Christian theology than in showing what was really there. So at the top of the map (the east, not the north) was Paradise; Jerusalem was at the centre. The three continents, Europe, Asia and Africa, were full of imaginary cities and mythical creatures.

In the 14th century, though Mediterranean pilots were still using portulans, the rediscovery of Ptolemy's maps provided a basis for a more accurate picture of the known world. Ptolemy believed that there had to be a large southern land-mass to balance the vast continents of the north. His theory excited many explorers, who longed to discover this new land.

Portulans were diagrams showing the outline of the coast, the position of harbours and the direction of the winds; they were the first versions of the marine charts used by later sailors. This map of the west coast of Morocco is part of an atlas drawn by Abraham Cresques in 1375, using the information provided by the portulans.

On medieval maps, the Earth is surrounded by the ocean, and divided by the T-shape formed by the Don, the Nile and the Mediterranean. Europe is on the left, Africa on the right; Asia is at the top, with Jerusalem at its centre.

Henry the Navigator

Henry the Navigator (1394-1460).
He himself went on few voyages, but he was a great patron of explorers.

The Portuguese conquest of the seas began with the capture of the Moorish castle of Ceuta, in North Africa, by Crusaders led by Don Henrique, a 19-year-old prince. When he returned to Portugal he settled at Sagres, a village on the Atlantic coast, and gathered together sailors, carpenters, ship-builders, astronomers and map-makers from all over Europe.

Henry the Navigator, as he became known, was determined to explore the coast of Africa, both to extend the Portuguese kingdom and to reduce the influence of the Muslims.

His first task was to persuade his sailors to go beyond Cape Bojador, in North-west Africa. It was generally believed that no one lived beyond this point, and that the seas were dangerously shallow and full of strong currents. It took 19 years, and 15 expeditions, before Gil Eannes sailed past this 'Cape of Fear' in 1432.

After that, the African coast was systematically explored, and trading-posts were established. By the time Henry died, as many as 25 of his caravels passed along the coast each year. The regions on the shores of West Africa were named after their products: Gold Coast, Slave Coast, Ivory Coast. After 1481, Portuguese interests were protected by a fortress at Mina, on the Gold Coast.

Henry's sailors used maps like this, showing the Mediterranean. They were instructed to bring home notes and sketches, so more accurate maps could be drawn.

An hour-glass was the only way of measuring time on board ship.

The Portuguese conquest of the ocean

The Portuguese used caravels to travel long distances across unknown seas. Caravels are not large, but they can sail close to the wind.

For the early explorers, the return journey was often more difficult than the outward one, because the wind was likely to be against them. The Portuguese had a bold new idea: they made their way home using favourable winds, even if this meant making long detours far from land. It was a much more efficient way of sailing, though the crew could become very anxious as they spent long weeks out of sight of land.

In 1484, Diogo Cão reached the mouth of the Congo. Four years later, Bartholomew Diaz became the first European to round the most southerly point in Africa, which he called the Cape of Storms; it is now known as the Cape of Good Hope.

The Portuguese staked their claim to a territory by erecting a stone cross, or *padrão*, which also served as a useful landmark.

Wind-roses were drawn on early maps to show where strong winds met.

A caravel is small but strong, riding high in the water, and carrying a crew of about twenty. It has two or three lateen sails, or sometimes two square and one lateen.

Vasco da Gama

Once Bartholomew Diaz had sailed round the south of Africa, it seemed possible that this could be a route to Asia which would open up the riches of the East to Portuguese traders.

On 8 July 1497, King Manuel I sent Vasco da Gama to try to reach the Spice Road via Africa. This was a bold venture, a journey to the other end of the known world. Da Gama had to work out his own route through seas ruled by Arab merchants; and he had to begin the process of colonising the country with a force of four ships and 170 men.

Vasco da Gama
(*c.* 1460-1524)

As well as its crew, each ship had to carry a great deal of equipment, including arms and ammunition, and spare sails and ropes. A great deal of food was also needed: dried meat and fish, dried peas, lard, wine, oil, water, flour, biscuits . . .

Da Gama and his men reached the Cape after 93 days at sea, and sailed up the east coast of Africa. Along the shore of Mozambique, they saw their first Arab dhows. Further north, at Malindi, da Gama recruited an Arab pilot who guided them to Calicut, on the south-west coast of India. They arrived there on 22 May 1498.

The return journey was a terrible ordeal; two-thirds of the crew died of scurvy. But the survivors were welcomed as heroes when they reached Lisbon, two years after their departure. The route to the Indies was now open.

Portuguese ships alongside an Arab dhow

An Indian woman carrying water

An Indian bazaar

The Portuguese in Asia

The Tower of Belem, at the entrance to Lisbon harbour

It took about fifty years for the Portuguese to colonise the lands found by Vasco da Gama.

Six months after da Gama returned to Portugal, Pedro Alvarez Cabral set out with a fleet of 13 ships. He established the first outpost in India of the Portuguese Empire when he set up a trading-post at Cochin in 1502. Only seven of his ships returned to Lisbon, but they brought back spices worth a fortune.

This wealth was used to send other expeditions to the east. Soon the Portuguese carracks ruled the Indian Ocean. The first Viceroy of India, Francisco de Almeida, waged a determined campaign against Arab shipping off the Malabar Coast. His successor, Albuquerque, conquered Hormuz in 1507, Goa in 1510, and

Ports in the Far East were very busy places.

Malacca in 1511. He set up a network of warehouses and strongholds at strategic points in this vast area. In 1533 the Portuguese settled in Macao, nearly into China; in 1543 they reached Japan.

Fishing with cormorants in Japan. The birds caught fish and brought them back to the boats.

How the Japanese saw the 'long-nosed' Portuguese. They called them 'barbarians'.

Pirates on the Malabar Coast

Portuguese carracks laden with treasure from the East, spices, precious stones and silks, made Lisbon the centre of the trade between Europe and Asia.

Christopher Columbus

Columbus had sailed over most of the known world, from the Arctic to the Equator. He was an experienced map-maker, and was familiar with all the latest discoveries so he felt confident he would reach his goal. Even the best geographers of that time underestimated the size of the Earth, and did not realise how much was covered by water. They had no idea there was a large landmass between the west of Europe and the east of Asia.

Christopher Columbus left Spain on 3 August 1492. The King and Queen of Spain had eventually agreed to pay for the expedition. He had struggled for ten years to obtain support in Portugal for his scheme: to sail west-wards to reach the eastern lands des-cribed by Marco Polo.

After a month at sea, the look-outs sighted land. The ships had reached the Bahamas.

The two caravels, the *Niña* and the *Pinta*, and Columbus' ship, the *Santa Maria*

Christopher Columbus (*c*. 1451-1506)

Columbus' fleet explored the coasts of Haiti and Cuba, which he called Cipangu, Marco Polo's name for Japan.

Christopher Columbus' coat of arms. The castle represents the kingdom of Castile, the lion the kingdom of Leon; the anchors show that he was an admiral, and the islands symbolise those he discovered.

The journey home through the winter storms was a terrifying experience, but Columbus finally reached Lisbon on 4 March 1493. He left 39 of his men on the island of Hispaniola (Haiti), with supplies of food and weapons to last them a year. They did not survive. Before Columbus returned they became involved in a frantic search for gold, which led to quarrels and murders.

This was the beginning of the story of the West Indies and the New World. But no one realised that Columbus had found a whole new continent. He

thought he had reached India and called the natives Indians. In fact it was America. He had also discovered the best way to get there by sea: via the Canary Islands.

Portugal now regretted its lack of support for Columbus, and wanted to stake a claim to some of the new territory, which was still thought to be the far east of Asia. In the end the Pope intervened. He decreed, in the Treaty of Tordesillas (1494), that the Earth should be divided along a line running north to south. The line ran 370 leagues west of the Cape Verde Islands off the west coast of Africa. Any new land to the east of this line was to belong to Portugal; anything to the west of it would be Spanish territory. This is why Portuguese is the language of Brazil, while Spanish is spoken everywhere else in South America.

Exploration was soon followed by conquest; wonder was replaced by brutality.

The pineapple was one of the first products to reach Europe from the New World.

Cabral's Portuguese expedition sailed for the West Indies in 1500, but was blown off course and discovered Brazil.

The New World

Columbus described in his diary the friendly people whom he found in the New World. He was struck by their gentle language, their ready smiles, and their complete lack of clothing.

An Algonquin chief

As explorers found more and more parts of the 'New World', they drew maps of the areas they discovered. The pieces were put together like a huge jigsaw puzzle, and the nature of the new continent began to emerge. Giovanni da Verrazano, writing in 1524, maintained that it covered a huge area, bigger than Europe or Africa, and almost as big as Asia. The name 'America' was chosen by a German publisher in honour of Amerigo Vespucci, whose account of his expedition had fired the public's imagination.

The discovery of America was not just a matter of geography; it was a cultural shock. For one thing, the Bible made no mention of this part of the world. When travellers saw the immense forests full of strange flowers, unknown animals, and peaceful people who never

wore clothes, some thought they had reached Paradise; though those who ended up at cannibal feasts probably doubted this.

People in Europe had to come to terms with a totally different culture. Some saw the 'Indians' as halfway between men and children, lacking in knowledge and sophistication. The philosopher Montaigne suggested that they were like 'wild' uncultivated plants compared to Europeans, the product of centuries of cultivation. Others regarded the Indians as near-animal. Even Columbus had remarked on their willingness to accept orders and to work for the explorers. Greed and the religious fanaticism of the conquerors reduced the native inhabitants to brutal slavery.

Columbus described the canoes used by the Indians.

Smoking was a local habit which the explorers found most intriguing.

Following the Spanish, the French, and the Dutch, English explorers arrived at an Algonquin village

The invasion of America

Part of the plan of
a fortress in Florida

Columbus' second voyage to America was a much larger expedition: 14 caravels, 3 carracks, and 1,500 men. The King of Spain wanted them to take firm control of the land already found, as well as making further explorations.

On his third voyage, in 1498, Columbus reached the Orinoco Delta in South America. After this, discoveries came quickly: Venezuela (1499), Brazil (1500), the Yucatan Peninsula (1507), Florida (1512) – the list went on and on.

Hundreds of adventurers excited about the New World went charging off into deserts and jungles in search of gold, careless of the intense heat, the

difficult terrain and the feuding between rival groups. Nothing, it seemed, could stop them.

The military conquest began in 1519, when Cortez attacked the Aztec Empire. This was the beginning of Spain's Golden Age.

An organization called the Casa de Contratación was set up in Seville, to control the trade between Europe and the New World. Hidden in its headquarters was a map, the *padron real*, to which all the most up-to-date information was added as it arrived; this map was used as the basis for seafarers' charts.

Silver and gold were carried by mule from the mines to the coast.

On the gold route, the heavy carracks were replaced by lofty galleons, which travelled across the Atlantic in huge convoys, sometimes up to 100 ships.

Around the world with Magellan

Ferdinand Magellan
(1480-1521)

The sailors found it
difficult to believe
that they would ever
reach the end of this
winding passage
between mountains.

Patagonia

Tierra del
Fuego

On 20 September 1519, five ships set
off from the south-west of Spain. They
were commanded by a Portuguese
captain, Fernão de Magalhais (in
English, Magellan), but his 250
sailors came from all around the
Mediterranean, from Portugal, Spain,
France, Greece and North Africa.
They were embarking on the most
daunting of voyages; all the way
round the world.

The journey across the Atlantic was
appalling. The ships had to weather
terrible storms, and the starving
crews, all suffering from scurvy,
became mutinous in the bitter cold.
But Magellan lived up to his reputa-
tion for battling on whatever hap-
pened, and after thirteen months the

ships sailed into what is now called Magellan's Strait, at the southern tip of South America. The eastern end of the Strait was easy to enter, but the sailors soon found themselves in a maze of channels between steep and windy mountains. It was 38 days before they emerged into the calm waters of the largest sea in the world, which they called the Pacific ('peaceful') Ocean.

By now, Magellan and his men had travelled 20,000 km. Their rations had run out long before, and they were surviving by eating rats and leather.

As his ships struggled through the Strait, Magellan saw fires burning on the land to the south. He called it Tierra del Fuego, the land of fire.

At last, in March 1521, they reached the island of Guam. Their supplies replenished, they sailed on to the Philippines, and there Magellan's luck ran out. He was killed by a local chieftain as he tried to negotiate an alliance with the ruler of Cebu, the principal trading port.

With Juan Sebastian de Elcano as captain in Magellan's place, the one remaining ship sailed back to Europe in 1522. Only 18 of the 250 sailors had survived. But they had sailed right round the world.

Magellan was killed by a poisoned javelin on the island of Mactan, just off Cèbu.

The Spaniards took possession of the Philippines in 1569.

The Galleon Route to Manila linked the Philippines and Acapulco, on the west coast of Mexico. From there, goods were carried overland to Veracruz, where they were loaded on to ships bound for Spain.

The exploration of Canada

Newfoundland cod-fisherman (1720)

In April 1524 Verrazano was sent by the French king, François I, to explore the North American coast. He made his landing where the city of New York now stands.

Cod-fishermen from Brittany already knew the seas between Newfoundland and Greenland, and in 1534 François sent Jacques Cartier there to explore the region and to prospect for

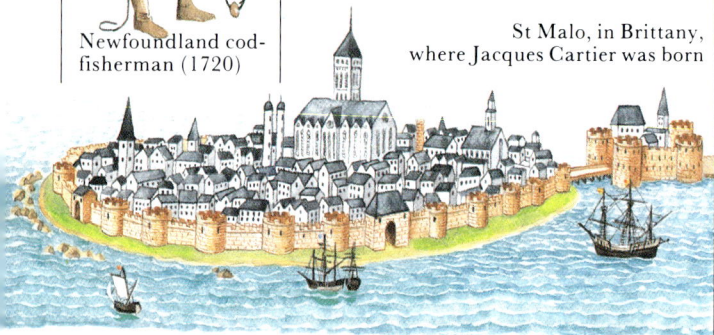

St Malo, in Brittany, where Jacques Cartier was born

gold. He also hoped to discover whether it was possible to sail round the northern tip of America to Asia.

On his first journey, Cartier explored the Gulf of St Lawrence, met several tribes of Indians, and claimed for France the land which the Indians called 'Canada'.

Cartier erecting a cross to show that Christians had landed

A year later he sailed further up the St Lawrence, to the village of Hochelaga, which he renamed Montreal, 'the king's mountain'. He made a third trip to Canada in 1541, but by then François I was losing interest in these expensive expeditions, which had failed to produce the promised gold and diamonds.

It was not until the next century that France again took an interest in North America, when Samuel du Champlain founded a French colony in Quebec.

The Belle Isle Strait between Labrador and Newfoundland.

'Signature' of an Iroquois chief (1710). Beavers were an important source of Canada's wealth; there was a flourishing trade in their skins.

Cartier's winter camp at Quebec in 1535. Below is his map of the St Lawrence.

SURE DE LA TERRE·NEVVE, GRANDE RIVIERE DE CANADA ET COTES DE L'OCEAN EN LA NOWELLE FRANCE

The North-west Passage

The early explorers were surprised to see white bears; and they were amazed when they saw them jump into the sea.

As early as the 16th century, the search began for a sea-passage to Asia round the northern coast of America. Magellan had discovered the southern passage, but the north proved a greater barrier. The way was obstructed by fog, icebergs, a mass of islands, and – worst of all – the pack-ice which covers much of the Arctic Ocean, especially in winter.

In 1610, Hudson explored the huge bay which is now named after him; but after a difficult winter the crew mutinied and abandoned Hudson, his

Hudson's ship in Hudson's Bay

son, and the seven seamen who supported them. They all died in the frozen wastes.

In 1615 and 1616, Baffin voyaged further north to Baffin Bay, but he too failed to find a passage through.

After this, European explorers lost interest in the problem; if the Northwest Passage was so difficult to find, it was unlikely to be useful for trade. It was almost three centuries before the Passage was finally discovered by the Norwegian explorer Amundsen in 1906.

Amundsen's ship, the *Gjoa*

Eskimo fishermen in their kayaks skim across the icy seas.

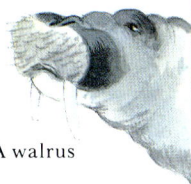

A walrus

In 1829, an English sailor made a wooden leg for an Eskimo bear-hunter.

The North-east Passage

Barents' ship caught in the ice

Building boats to escape. In the background is the cabin where the sailors spent the winter.

The shortest route from Europe to Asia passes over the North Pole. So while the search continued for the North-west Passage, other explorers were trying to find a way east from the seas of northern Europe.

In 1594, a Dutchman called Willem Barents reached Novaya Zemlya. The following year he set off for China, his seven ships laden with goods, but the pack-ice forced him to give up. He reached Spitzbergen a year later, but this time the ice trapped his ship. Having survived the polar winter, he died the following summer, in June 1597, as he and his surviving men were escaping in makeshift boats made out of wood salvaged from the ship.

Barents' ill-fated voyage had an unexpected consequence. The discovery that the seas around Spitzbergen were full of whales began an 'oil-rush' which lasted throughout the 17th century, as whalers jostled to share in the riches.

In 1725, the Tsar of Russia sent Vitus Bering to search for the elusive North-east Passage. Sailing from the east coast of Siberia in 1728, Bering found the Strait named after him; but he could go no further.

The Passage was eventually found in 1878, by the Swedish explorer Nordenskjöld on board the *Vega*.

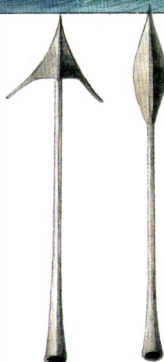

Dutch whalers and their harpoons in the 17th century

PACIFIC OCEAN

Bering Strait

JAPAN

ALASKA

SIBERIA

CHINA

NORTH POLE

Hudson's Bay

SPIZTBERGEN ISLES

NOVAYA ZEMLYA

NORTH AMERICA

GREENLAND

Amundsen's journey (North-west)

ICELAND

Nordenskjöld's journey (North-east)

NEWFOUNDLAND

BRITISH ISLES

EUROPE

53

Australasia

The second voyage round the world was made by Sir Francis Drake between 1577 and 1580. By then, the vast oceans discovered by Magellan were busy highways for merchant-ships and warships.

The rest of Europe followed Spain and Portugal into the spice trade and the rush to claim colonies. The East India Company was founded in 1600, and the Dutch East India Company in 1602. The power of these two companies, which controlled trading-posts on all the sea-routes of Asia and Europe, forced everyone else to find other routes.

Because of this, in 1616 two Dutch captains, Le Maire and Schouten, set off in search of a route to the south of Magellan's Strait, and sailed right round Cape Horn. It was much more dangerous than the Strait, but also a great deal faster.

The natives of the New Hebrides were drawn by an artist on an expedition to the South Seas in 1605.

The huge albatross, like the dolphin, was thought to be the sailor's friend.

In the middle of the 17th century another Dutch captain, Abel Tasman, was commissioned by the Dutch East India Company to find the legendary southern continent. He was the first European to discover New Zealand and Tasmania.

The Dutch East India Company took little interest in the lands which Tasman found; at the time they seemed unlikely to have any commercial importance.

The South Seas

For the great trading companies, the purpose of seafaring was commerce and profit. The magnificent ships of the 17th century rarely strayed from the main shipping-routes, which made use of the prevailing winds. No one was interested in financing a voyage of discovery; an expedition was expensive, and the new lands usually had little to offer in comparison with the riches of the East and West Indies.

Pirates lay in wait on the trade-routes, around the coast of Madagascar, in the West Indies and on the China Seas. Their swashbuckling brutality became part of seafaring folklore. Stories of adventures at sea began to take the place of fantastic 'travellers' tales': Defoe's *Robinson Crusoe*, for instance, is based on the true story of Alexander Selkirk. The discovery of 'new worlds', too, fired

Sailors filling casks with fresh water

In 1708 a Scottish sailor, Alexander Selkirk, was rescued from the island of Juan Fernandez, where he had lived alone for four years. He was the original Robinson Crusoe.

The people of Melanesia and Polynesia were remarkable sailors who steered by the stars.

Their boats were outrigger canoes with a single sail.

the imagination of writers like Thomas More, who wrote *Utopia* in 1516, and Jonathan Swift, author of *Gulliver's Travels* (1726).

Flying fish

The South Seas were so different from Europe that they seemed to belong in the realms of fantasy.

After months at sea, land was a very welcome sight; it meant the ship could be restocked with drinking water and fresh provisions.

Scientific exploration

An octant, made in England in about 1680. With this instrument, it was possible to calculate latitude to within a kilometre.

Gutenberg's Bible, the first printed book, appeared in 1454, almost 40 years before Columbus reached America. As explorers pushed back the boundaries of the known world, more and more books were being produced, and stories, maps and pictures of the new worlds found their way into the libraries of scholars and interested amateurs.

In the 18th century learned societies, such as the Royal Society in London and the French Académie, encouraged all kinds of scientific and technological research which might

The learned societies had foreign correspondents in every part of Europe.

lead to further discoveries. The best available craftsmen were employed to design and make new instruments which would be more accurate and more reliable. By the end of the 18th

Earlier accounts of voyages were examined critically, to remove exaggerations and misleading information. The men of Patagonia, for example, whom one of Magellan's crew had described as giants, turned out to be of quite normal size.

Sketches were sometimes better than words.

century, all official expeditions were for scientific purposes.

Artists, botanists and naturalists set sail in the new 'laboratory ships'. Back in Europe, natural history museums were set up to display specimens from the unknown lands. Those who stayed at home reflected upon the origins of 'civilised' man. The first encyclopaedia was produced in France around this time.

Melanesian lances. Many of the early museums contained a great assortment of objects from all over the world.

59

The first modern maps

In 1569 the art of map-making was revolutionised. Gerhard Mercator devised what is still called Mercator's projection. Earlier map-makers overcame the difficulty of drawing the Earth's curved surface on a flat piece of paper, by distorting the lines of latitude and longitude.

New Holland

Van Diemen's Land (Tasmania)

New Guinea

New Holland

New South Wales

AUSTRALIA

New Zealand

Van Diemen's Land (Tasmania)

The upper map shows Australia as it was drawn in about 1750. New Zealand is part of a huge southern continent, and New Guinea is joined on to Australia. The first map to show New Zealand in the right place was drawn by Captain Cook in 1770. The red line shows his route.

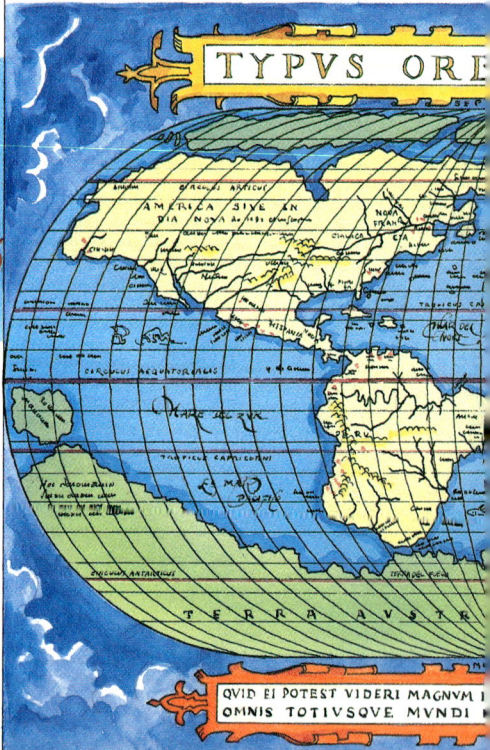

TYPVS ORB

CIRCVLVS ARTICVS

AMERICA SIVE IN

DIA NOVA

NOVA SPANIA

CIRCVLVS AEQVINOCTIALIS

TROPICO CA

TROPICVS CAPRICORNI

CIRCVLVS ANTARTICVS

TERRA AVSTR

QVID EI POTEST VIDERI MAGNVM I
OMNIS TOTIVSQVE MVNDI

Bougainville

Cook

La Pérouse

Mercator drew them parallel, which distorted the relative sizes of the continents and oceans, but allowed sailors to plot their courses with straight lines, rather than curves.

By the 18th century, most of the world was known; only the southernmost continent remained a mystery.

These three men led major scientific expeditions in the eighteenth century.

Abraham Ortelins published this map in 1570. It is part of the first attempt to produce a scientific atlas.

The huge land-mass at the bottom of the map, described as 'southern land as yet unknown', includes Tierra del Fuego and New Guinea. Explorers struggled to work out the shape of this land-mass; we now known that there are in fact two large areas (Australia and Antarctica), and many smaller islands.

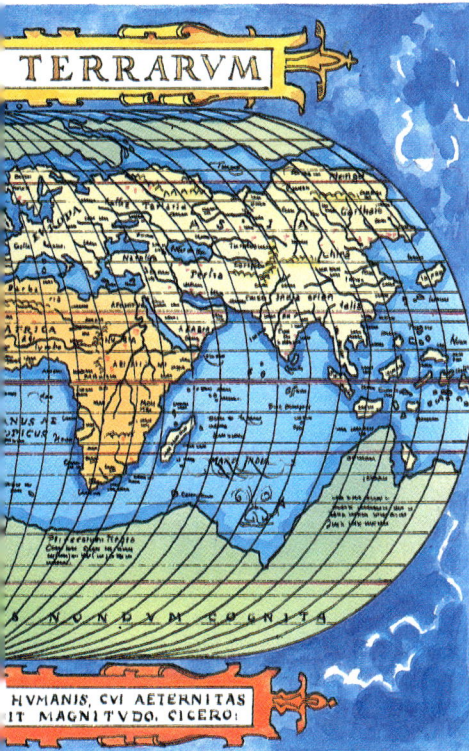

Bougainville and the garden of Eden

Bougainvillaea, a climbing plant discovered in Brazil by Philibert Commerson

On 4 April 1768, two French ships anchored at Tahiti; the sea was covered with canoes full of people waving palm branches to welcome them.

Bougainville was overwhelmed by what he saw. He was so struck by the beauty and friendliness of the inhabitants, that he named the island the 'new Cythera', after the Greek island said to be the birthplace of the goddess Aphrodite.

His companions on the voyage included the naturalist Philibert Commerson, the astronomer Véron, and a crew of 400. They all felt that they had reached some kind of earthly paradise.

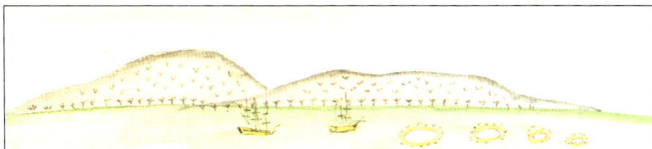

Philosophers of the time were intrigued by the idea of the 'noble savage': a man without a European intellectual education who was nonetheless morally admirable. Bougainville thought that he had found such a people in Tahiti, and hoped that their society could remain undisturbed.

But he was soon disillusioned by Aoturu, a young chieftain who returned to Europe with the French ships. Aoturu explained that Tahiti too had slavery and endless wars.

Sketch-map of the island of Tahiti

Bougainville brought back this funeral robe belonging to a Tahitian priest.

Captain Cook

The *Endeavour*, Cook's ship, was originally used to transport coal, but Cook's modifications turned it into an excellent vessel for exploration.

A Maori and an Englishman bartering

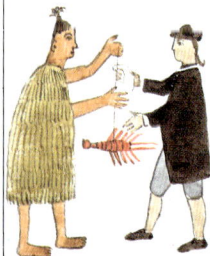

James Cook was the son of a Scottish farm-labourer, and first went to sea when he was 18. By the time the Admiralty put him in charge of a scientific expedition to the southern hemisphere, he was a thoroughly experienced sea farer. His orders were to go first to Tahiti to watch the planet Venus pass in front of the sun on 3 June 1769, and then to find the southern

The Maoris, the original inhabitants of New Zealand, were cannibal warriors who decorated their faces with elaborate tattoos.

continent, if it existed. He was accompanied by a team of distinguished botanists eager to collect exotic plants, fruits and shrubs. Cook went to New Zealand, sailed right round both North and South Islands, and surveyed their coasts. He then explored the east coast of Australia, where he damaged his ship on the coral of the Great Barrier Reef.

While the ship was being repaired, the naturalists on board were able to continue their work, studying everything from gum-trees to kangaroos. They collected over 700 species of plants.

Cook was the first sea-captain to overcome scurvy by insisting that his men eat fresh fruit and vegetables. But on the way back to England the *Endeavour* stopped at Djakarta, where 30 of the crew died of malaria and dysentery.

Captain Cook and his men spent more than a month in Australia after their ship was holed on the Great Barrier Reef, a vast expanse of coral which stretches along almost 2,000 km of the coast.

The ship needed very thorough repair if it was to survive storms like this on the way back to Europe.

Cook's later voyages

Chin-strap penguin

Captain Cook's second and third voyages of discovery took him to the two ends of the Earth. Between 1772 and 1774, the *Resolution* and the *Adventure* sailed as far south as they could, but were eventually stopped by the pack-ice, rather to the relief of the crew. They sailed right round the south of the world, but failed to find the Antarctic mainland. Cook then explored the Pacific, and discovered (or rediscovered) various islands: the Friendly Islands (Tonga), Easter Island, the Marquesas, and the New Hebrides.

In 1776 he set off again, with the *Resolution* and the *Discovery*, this time in search of the North-west Passage. He discovered Hawaii and the Aleutian Islands on his way, but had to turn back after the Bering Strait because of the ice. He stopped again at Hawaii on his way home. There, he was tragically killed in a clash with the natives.

An 'Indian' from the Aleutian Islands in his canoe

The chronometer, made by John Harrison, which Captain Cook took on his voyages. With it he was able to measure longitude really accurately.

Captain Cook's death in Hawaii on 14 February 1779. He was revered as a god by the Hawaiians for years after his death.

The pursuit of knowledge

The giant statues on Easter Island fascinated explorers. La Pérouse measured some of them.

On 13 July 1786, six officers and fifteen seamen drowned off the coast of Alaska. They belonged to an expedition led by La Pérouse, which had set off, on the *Astrolabe* and the *Boussole* ('compass'), to explore the northern coasts of America and Asia.

Two years later 32 members of the expedition were killed or wounded on Samoa, in a battle with the inhabitants. La Pérouse left his record of the voyage in the safe keeping of an English ship, and set sail for Tonga. After that, the expedition simply disappeared . . .

In 1791, two French ships set off to look for La Pérouse, but failed to find him. The rescue party suffered from scurvy, dysentery and various fevers, and fierce political arguments also broke out, since this was only two years after the French Revolution.

Finally, in 1828, Dumont d'Urville
discovered that La Pérouse's ships
had been wrecked off Vanikoro, in the
South Pacific.

All these expeditions did research.
La Pérouse had been accompanied by
17 scientists, artists and scholars. The
work of Dumont d'Urville's team filled
14 books and 5 atlases; there were
12,000 drawings, and many specimens
of flora and fauna.

Bird of paradise

Dumont d'Urville's
Astrolabe. He went on
exploring until 1840,
and discovered
Adélie Land, in
Antarctica.

Map of the main voyages of discovery

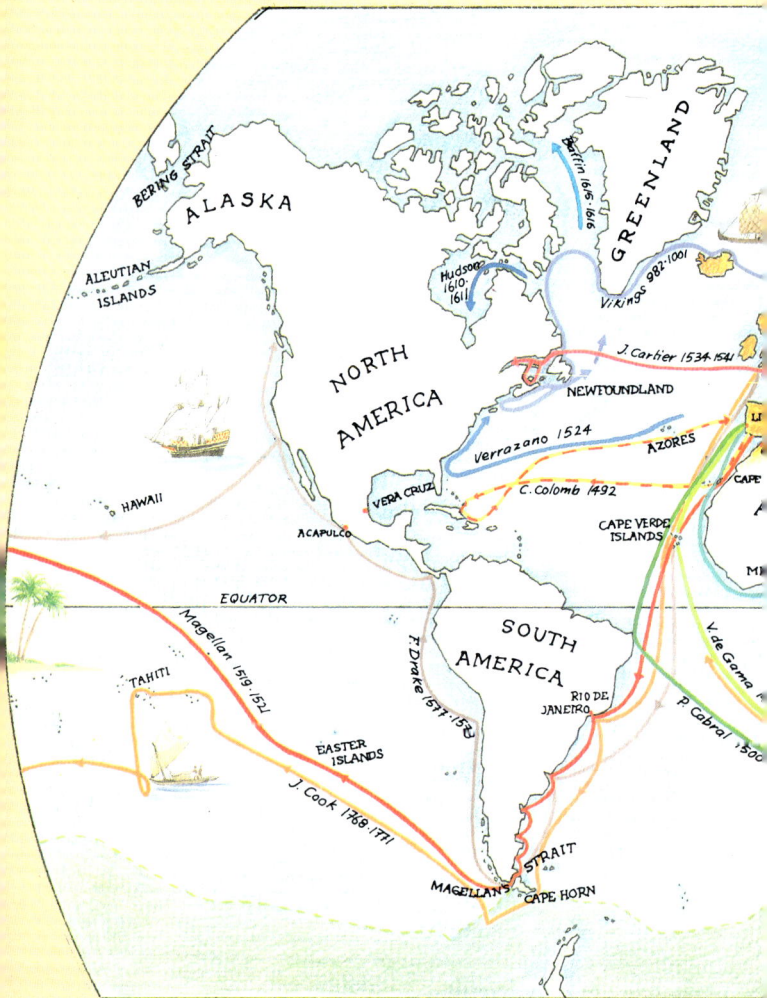

BERING STRAIT

ALASKA

ALEUTIAN ISLANDS

NORTH AMERICA

HAWAII

ACAPULCO

VERA CRUZ

GREENLAND

Baffin 1615-1616

Hudson 1610-1611

Vikings 982-1001

J. Cartier 1534-1541

NEWFOUNDLAND

Verrazano 1524

C. Colomb 1492

AZORES

CAPE VERDE ISLANDS

CAPE

LI

A

M

EQUATOR

Magellan 1519-1521

TAHITI

EASTER ISLANDS

J. Cook 1768-1771

SOUTH AMERICA

F. Drake 1577-1580

RIO DE JANEIRO

V. de Gama

P. Cabral 1500

MAGELLAN'S STRAIT

CAPE HORN

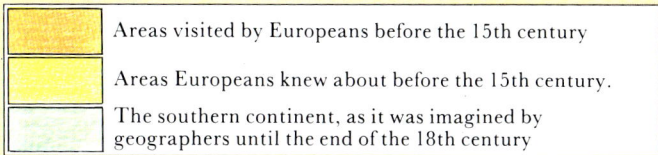

Areas visited by Europeans before the 15th century

Areas Europeans knew about before the 15th century.

The southern continent, as it was imagined by geographers until the end of the 18th century

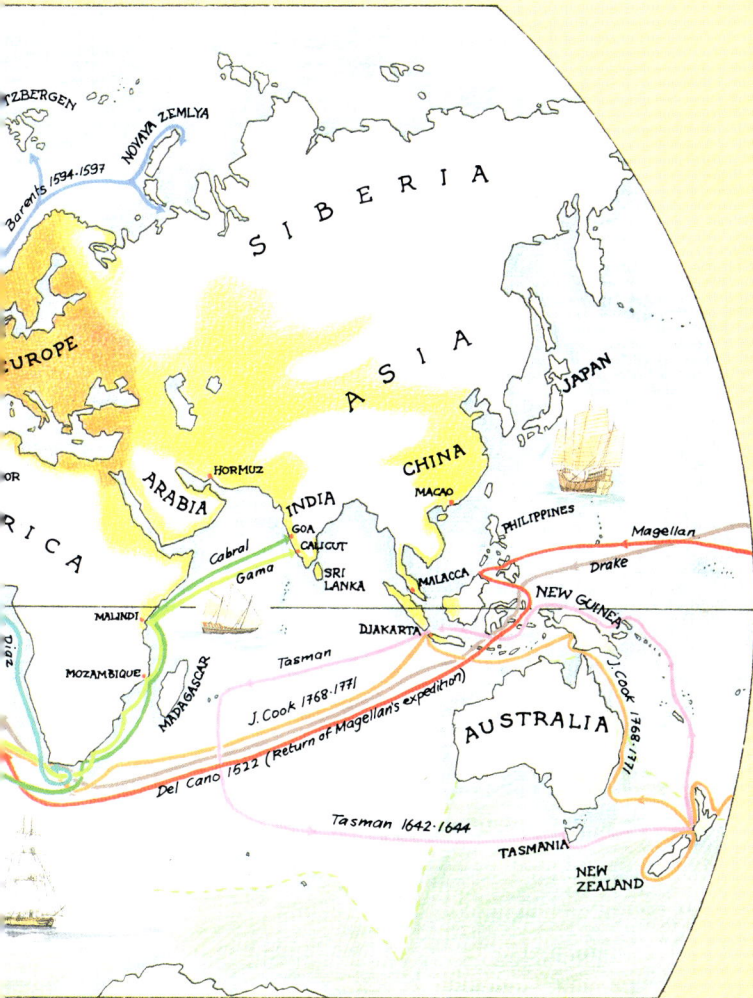

*They are ill discoverers that think
there is no land when they
can see nothing but sea.*

Francis Bacon
(1561-1626)

An A to Z of Exploration

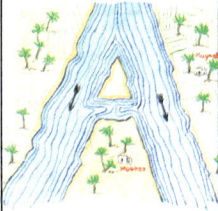

Antarctic
The most southerly part of the earth, with the South Pole at its centre. The Antarctic Circle goes round the earth at 66°32′ S.

Arctic
The most northerly part of the Earth. There is no Arctic continent, just frozen sea and some islands.

Bojador (Cape)
On the north-west coast of Africa. It was for many years the most southerly point visited by Europeans.

Bronze
A mixture of copper and tin. The need for tin was the cause of some of the earliest voyages of discovery; later explorers went in search of precious metals.

Caravel
A light carvel-built sailing ship (carvel and caravel are versions of the same word); it had one or more triangular lateen sails, and was easy to manoeuvre.

Carrack
A heavy cargo ship, with several masts.

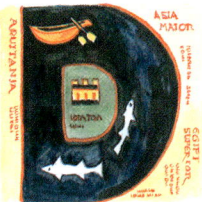

Dhow
Arab ship which sailed in the Red Sea and the Indian Ocean.

Equator
An imaginary line drawn round the Earth, halfway between the two Poles; it therefore divides the earth into two equal hemispheres, northern and southern.

Fog
This was a major problem for early sailors, who could not navigate without the sun or stars.

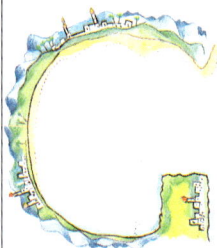

Galleon
From the 16th
century, these large
sailing-ships were
used to carry goods
between America and
Spain.

Galley
A ship which had
several banks of oars
as well as sails; often
rowed by slaves.

Hanse
A league of
merchants in
northern Europe;
the Hanse had a
virtual monopoly of
sea-borne trade.

Horn (Cape)
The south end of the
Tierra del Fuego. It is
a cliff some 600 m
high, overlooking a
very dangerous sea.

Incognita (Terra)
Land which is known
or believed to exist,
although it has not
yet been explored.

Indies
The East Indies were
all the countries in
Asia which traded
with Europe: India,
China, Ceylon (Sri
Lanka), etc. The
West Indies were
originally the trading
countries in America,
and included Brazil,
Mexico and Peru.

Junk
Far Eastern sailing-
ship. Its sails are
made of cloth

stitched on to hori-
zontal bamboo rods.

Latitude
Distance from the
equator, measured in
degrees rather than
in kilometres.

Longitude
Distance from the
Greenwich
Meridian, again
measured in degrees.

Meridian
Imaginary circle
on the earth which
passes through both
poles.

Monsoon
Predictable system of
winds which change
direction suddenly at
different times of the
year, to give a wet
season and a dry one.

Myths

Stories which offer an explanation of the world; they are widely believed to be true by the people who devise them. They frequently concern fabulous people or animals.

Norsemen

The Vikings were also known as Northmen, Norsemen or (later) Normans; all these names mean the same.

Octant

Instrument used to measure the height of a star above the horizon; it was later replaced by the sextant.

Parallel

Imaginary circle parallel with the equator.

Poles

The points at the two ends of the earth's axis.

Quest

A journey to find a specific place or object.

Rose

A windrose is the star formed by the four cardinal points (north, east, south and west) and the intermediate wind-directions.

Scurvy

Disease caused by lack of Vitamin C in the diet. The best source of Vitamin C is fresh fruit and vegetables, difficult to store on a long sea voyage.

Tropics

Two imaginary circles parallel with the equator and at a distance of 23°27′ from it.

The Tropic of Cancer is in the northern hemisphere and the Tropic of Capricorn in the south.
A tropical climate is always hot.

Utopia
An imaginary island invented by Sir Thomas More. It is surrounded by a dangerous sea, and is the home of happy people ruled by an ideal government.

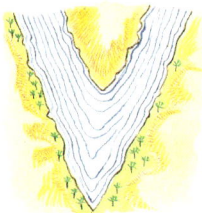

Volta
A method of sailing perfected by the Portuguese. Instead of trying to travel the shortest possible distance, they made use of the winds to arrive at their destination as fast as possible.

Zenith
The highest point in the sky reached by the sun or a star.

About the Author and Illustrator

François Place was born in 1957, and has lived in Paris since 1974. He studied at art school, and has made his living since then as an illustrator and graphic designer. He has illustrated the companion volume to this book, *Conquerors and Invaders*, as well as *Living in Ancient Rome* (a 'Pocket Worlds'). He has not personally travelled widely but says that he travels in the imagination through the antiquarian books and maps he uses for his illustrations.

I dedicate this book to my parents.

Other titles in the *Discoverers* series:

Discovering the seasons:

Spring
Summer
Autumn
Winter

Discovering nature:

Your Cat
The Book of the Sky
The Book of Rivers
The Book of the Forest
The Book of Deserts
The Book of Mountains
Flowers

Discovering history:

Painting and Painters
The Book of Inventions and Discoveries
Clothes Through the Ages
Uniforms Through the Ages
Ships and Seafarers
Conquerors and Invaders
Navigators and Explorers

Discovering transport:

The Book of Trains
The History of Aviation, Vol.1

Discovering art:

Painting and Painters